Ghosts of Gold is the story of First Nations man, Jupiter Mosman, who discovered gold at Charters Towers in North Queensland, Australia.

READ about the discovery of gold at Charters Towers and how this goldfield in the years 1872 to 1917 became Australia's largest high-grade gold producer.

FIND OUT about Jupiter Mosman, his life, final years, and his experience with discrimination and injustice

LEARN about the land of opportunity on the northern frontier and how it was taken over by British pastoralists and miners

UNCOVER the meaning of the policy of "dispersal" and its associated campaign of frontier violence against First Nations people

DISCOVER the birth of Charters Towers, some of its stories, epic overland cattle drives, and the work of drovers like Jupiter Mosman

and much more...

Gold! Hidden Stories of Australia s Past, Book 4

Ghosts of Gold

The Life and Times of Jupiter Mosman

Marji Hill

Published by The Prison Tree Press 2022
Suite 124, 1-10 Albert Avenue, Broadbeach, Queensland 4218
https://marjihill.com   https://www.fastselfpublishing.com
Copyright © 2022 Marji Hill
Copyright © 2022 Artwork and paintings by Marji Hill
Editor: Eddie Dowd
Cover image *Early Charters Towers Goldfield* is a gouache painting on paper by Marji Hill
Jupiter's Lucky Strike, oil painting by Marji Hill is held by the Citigold Corporation
The portrait of *Jupiter Mosman* painted by Marji Hill hangs in the World Theatre at Charters Towers

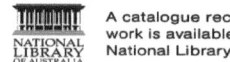
A catalogue record for this work is available from the National Library of Australia

ISBN 978-0-6454834-6-8 (paperback)
ISBN 978-0-6454834-7-5 (eBook)

All rights reserved. No part of this book may be reproduced, stored in a retrieval system, or transmitted in any form or by any means, electronic, mechanical, photocopying, recording, scanning, or otherwise, without the prior written permission of the publisher.

Disclaimer

All the material contained in this book is provided for educational and informational purposes only. No responsibility can be taken for any results or outcomes resulting from the use of this material.

While every care has been taken to trace and acknowledge copyright the publishers tender their apologies for any accidental infringement where copyright has proved untraceable.

Every attempt has been made to provide information that is both accurate and effective, however, the author does not assume any responsibility for the accuracy or use/misuse of this information.

WARNING: Aboriginal and Torres Strait Islander people are advised that this book contains images and names of people who have passed away.

THE SERIES

Gold! Hidden Stories of Australia's Past

Book 1
The Gates of Gold:
The Discovery of Gold, its Legacy and Australian Identity

Book 2
Shadows of Gold:
Eureka and the Birth of Australian democracy

Book 3
Gold and the Chinese:
Racism, Riots and Protest on the Australian Goldfields

Book 4
Ghosts of Gold:
The Life and Times of Jupiter Mosman

Book 5
Blood Gold:
Native Police, Bushrangers & Lawlessness on the Australian Goldfields

DEDICATION

In memory of
Alex Barlow

TABLE OF CONTENTS

Preface	xiii
Chapter 1 - High Grade Goldfield	1
Chapter 2 - Land of Opportunity	9
Chapter 3 - Frontier Violence	17
Chapter 4 - The Mosmans	25
Chapter 5 - Gold	35
Chapter 6 - The "World"	41
Chapter 7 - Away from the Golden Frenzy	57
Chapter 8 - Droving Days	63
Chapter 9 - Service to the Cattle Industry	79
Chapter 10 - A Man of Dignity	91
Sources	101
Questions For Further Consideration	105
About Marji Hill	107
More Books by Marji Hill	113

ACKNOWLEDGEMENTS

I acknowledge the Traditional Custodians of Country throughout Australia and their connections to land, sea, and community. I pay my respect to elders, past, present, and emerging and extend my respect to all First Nations peoples today.

In particular, I acknowledge the Gudjal people who for tens of thousands of years, lived in the Charters Towers region. I also acknowledge their neighbours - the Gugu Badhun, Yirandali and Jangga people.

In the spirit of reconciliation, my mission is to increase understanding between the First Nations and other Australians and to provide people from all over the globe with a basic understanding of Australia's first people, their history, and cultures.

In my life, I've been fortunate to have had several mentors. Alex Barlow, my late partner, would always say to me "If you manage your time well, you can achieve everything you want in life." That started my quest into the world of time management and learning how to maximise my productivity.

John Foley, a barrister, helped me to expand my vision and has inspired me to make possible what seemed impossible. Sherien Foley has always been there to challenge and kickstart me and I remember her words when I hit rock bottom with my work many years ago she said to me "There's only one way to go and that's up!"

This current series of books about gold grew out of a brainstorming session I had with my old friend, Gail Parr while staying with her and her husband, George Sansbury at Maryborough in Queensland. We thrashed out the concept and from this grew these five books.

I would also like to acknowledge the late and great Jim Lynch who introduced me to the Charters Towers gold story many years ago and to his, son, Mark Lynch, Chairperson of the Citigold Corporation, who has always supported and encouraged my creativity in relation to the gold story both in books and in art.

And finally, thank you, Eddie Dowd, my backstop and mentor, who has helped me get my books into their final form and ready for publication.

Marji Hill

Preface

In January 1997 my late partner, Alex Barlow and I made a memorable trip to Charters Towers in North Queensland.

My goal was to make a series of paintings based on the Charters Towers goldfield. We stayed in an old Queenslander - backpackers accommodation in Charters Towers.

Being January, the heat was extreme. The road outside was so hot you could have fried an egg on the bitumen. My attempt at painting during the day was impossible. It was far too hot. I reverted to plan B and decided to do my painting in *plein air* just after sunrise.

Because of the extreme heat, the painting experience was uncomfortable. I had to paint fast so that I could return to the air-conditioning of the backpackers to escape the heat.

Over the two weeks that we were in Charters Towers I made a series of about ten small, gouache paintings that were exhibited down south at a Canberra gallery.

During our time at Charters Towers, Alex and I came across a small, archival photograph of Jupiter Mosman.

This find stirred our interest in Jupiter. Alex began researching the Jupiter Mosman story and he started connecting with some of the people who had been associated with him. While he did the research into Jupiter Mosman, I painted Jupiter's portrait.

The Citigold Corporation then commissioned me to make a painting about the discovery of gold at Charters Towers.

This was *Jupiter's Lucky Strike* which celebrates the discovery of gold by First Nations boy, Jupiter Mosman in 1871 at Charters Towers in North Queensland.

The painting today is in Charters Towers and hangs in the Citigold Corporation office.

For many years the painting hung in the foyer of Jupiter's Casino in Townsville but when the casino was sold, becoming The Ville Resort-Casino, the painting went to its home in Charters Towers.

The Jupiter Mosman portrait hangs in the World Theatre at Charters Towers.

As a result of Alex Barlow's research, we drafted the Jupiter Mosman story but sadly, Alex passed away in November 2012.

This current book, *The Ghosts of Gold: The Life and Times of Jupiter Mosman*, came into being as a result of the research that Alex did and it is based on the original draft manuscript that we created.

Marji Hill

"The Charters Towers goldfield from 1872 to 1917 was Australia's largest high-grade gold producer of 6,600,000 ounces of gold ore averaging 38g/t (near 2 ounces per ton of ore)"

Citigold Corporation

Chapter 1 - High Grade Goldfield

J upiter Mosman, a ten-year-old First Nations boy, discovered gold at Charters Towers in North Queensland in 1871.

The Charters Towers goldfield from 1872 to 1917 was Australia s largest high-grade gold producer of 6,600,000 ounces of gold ore averaging 38 grams/ton (near 2 ounces per ton of ore). These gold mines of the past were profitable and they paid out an estimated one billion dollars in dividends to their shareholders, in today s dollars [1].

The Charters Towers goldfield today is centred on and around the town of Charters Towers in North Queensland which is 128 kilometres from the coastal city of Townsville.

The grade represented the largest gold-producing field in Queensland, and it comprised 36 per cent of the state s total gold production.

---

[1] Citigold Corporation https://www.citigold.com/

The quality of the gold ore grade from the Charters Towers mines was estimated to be almost double that of the Victorian goldfields and almost 75 percent higher than the grades of Western Australian (Kalgoorlie) goldfields at that time [2].

Finding gold

On 23 December 1871 at what became Charters Towers there was a threat to storm on a mid-summer evening. Three gold prospectors and their First Nations boy were preparing to set up camp close to the high, rocky, tower-like formation.

From a distance, this rock formation looked like the tors (rocky outcrops) so often seen in England.

The prospectors were Hugh Mosman, George Clarke and James Fraser.

The First Nations' boy was called Jupiter Mosman.

Before they could unload their pack-horse a terrific clap of thunder frightened it. The horse galloped away into the bush.

With it went all their cooking gear and most of their supplies.

---

[2] Citigold Corporation https://www.citigold.com/

Construction of the modern decline at Charters Towers

There was little talk among the prospectors as they hurried to set up camp and get a fire started to boil their billies and to get some food cooked before the storm hit.

Soon the thunder and the lightning rolled and flashed over them and a heavy downpour of rain soaked them and all the bush around them.

When daylight came the prospectors were anxious to find the spooked horse and the equipment that it had carried away.

The care of the horses was Jupiter's job.

Whilst the prospectors tidied up the camp and hung clothes and ground sheets out to dry, Jupiter went tracking to look for signs of the horse.

The storm had set little rivulets of water flowing down the gullies from the hillside near where they had camped. Jupiter found the horse at the base of the hillside, grazing near one of these rivulets.

Having tethered the horse, he knelt by the freshwater stream to scoop up a drink. As he did so he saw the early morning sunlight glistening on a small stone in the water.

Jupiter's Lucky Strike

Gold! Hidden Stories of Australia s Past,
Book 4

Jupiter had been on the goldfields here in North Queensland long enough to know gold when he saw it. Jumping with excitement he raced back to the campsite shouting to Hugh Mosman and the others to come and see, Gold! Gold! Gold!"

It was Christmas Eve, 24 December 1871.

The claims

When Jupiter Mosman discovered gold at Charters Towers he was about ten years old.

In the next few days Mosman, Clarke and Fraser staked out three rich reefs near the hill which they had named Towers Hill. These claims became known as the North Australian, General Wyndham and Washington.

The three prospectors were in a rush to register their claims. The nearest Mining Warden, the Gold Commissioner, was at Ravenswood. His name was Mr. W.S.E.M. Charters.

On 2 January 1872, the claims were registered. The new goldfield, which was called Charters Tors was named after the Gold Commissioner. The name later changed to Charters Towers.

The Charters Towers goldfield was officially proclaimed on 26 February 1872.

Gold! Hidden Stories of Australia s Past,
Book 4

"Prior to the British takeover of lands in this new continent, First Nations people had defined territories.

They knew the boundaries of their traditional country."

Marji Hill

Chapter 2 - Land of Opportunity

Jupiter Mosman was probably born in 1861.

In that same year explorer, George Dalrymple (1826-1876) organised an expedition to explore the Burdekin River watershed (Kennedy district). The area was recognised as a land of opportunity for the British newcomers and was thought to have enormous potential for sheep grazing.

Dalrymple led a large group of pioneer pastoralists from Rockhampton north to Port Denison. In his expedition party were twenty-four pioneers who were coming to find land on which to settle. There was also a unit of the Native Mounted Police, a dozen First Nations troopers, two sergeants and their officers.

All up the expedition party consisted of forty-two men and one hundred and fifty horses. There were also cattle to slaughter for meat along the way and a small dairy herd.

In the last days of March in 1861, Dalrymple's expedition party had been preceded by three small ships which arrived in Port Denison. On board were the new Harbour Master, the Customs Officer and the Clerk of Petty Sessions.

The ships carried thirty-three people including wives and children. On instructions from Dalrymple, they did not go ashore to the mainland. Instead, they set up camp on Stone Island in the middle of the harbour.

They watched

A large group of armed First Nations men seeing the ships sail into the harbour had gathered on the shore. There they remained and watched. They did not attack these newcomers to their home country. They watched to see if there was to be any kind of threat.

By this time in North Queensland, First Nations people had heard of these strange new, white people.

From a First Nations perspective, these people with their pale faces had arrived with hundreds of large, strange-looking animals that messed up the waterholes. The animals drank them dry and all the food plants on which people relied were eaten.

Kangaroos and other native animals were killed off. Even people were killed. The white newcomers had what looked like long sticks which puffed smoke, made a large clap and put holes in people.

The white people stole tools like spears and boomerangs and boats. They took women and children away to live with them.

All of this they had heard from their own people who had seen or heard about these things as they travelled the trade routes to the great ceremonial meetings that brought people together from the many different traditional lands.

First Nations Gia people and some of their friends from the nearby Juru people watched.

Bowen

When the overland party arrived at what was named the settlement of Bowen, the horsemen were drawn up on a small rise above the beach. Volleys were fired into the air.

This announced the arrival of the British. It was also to frighten off any local First Nations people who might still be hiding in the nearby bush.

The next day a settlement was officially proclaimed. The British flag was hoisted and the new settlement of Bowen came into being.

In the days that followed a township emerged.

Within days the British newcomers began to move out into the countryside. They explored the county for suitable grazing land on which to establish their sheep and cattle runs.

Everywhere along the rivers and creeks they found large groups of Gia and Juru people.

Prior to the British takeover of land in this new continent, First Nations people had defined territories.

They knew the boundaries of their traditional Country. They knew its physical features, geography, animals, birds, fish and plants. They looked after their lands and they ritually cared for their Country with ceremony, songs, stories, and art.

The British settlers were afraid that these local inhabitants might attack them. This had already happened in other parts of Australia when settlers had tried to open up new territories.

The new township of Bowen was really an armed camp. Cannon had been brought ashore from the ships and everyone was armed with pistols and muskets.

Dalrymple requested, in his first report to the colonial government in Brisbane, that more police be sent to the town.

Besides the many First Nations inhabitants that they encountered the British came across pioneer settlers who had preceded them into this newly opened up country.

Besides the many First Nations inhabitants that they encountered the British came across pioneer settlers who had preceded them into this newly opened up country.

One of them was Christopher Allingham. He had driven sheep and cattle from Armidale in the colony of New South Wales and he settled close to Bowen on the Don River.

As soon as the British newcomers believed that Bowen was secure from an attack by the local First Nations people, several of them with Allingham and a First Nations man whom they called 'Jimmy', set out from the town to look for territory to open up.

Two of the British party were attacked by Gia warriors. One of them was knocked off his horse and unconscious. The other killed several of the warriors with his pistols and drove the rest away.

The explorers went over the Burdekin River, through a gap in the Leichardt Range, went on to where the Burdekin joined the Suttor River and then to the Cape River.

Phillip Somer, who had been knocked unconscious in the earlier affray with Gia warriors, marked out for himself a 200,000 acre (nearly 81,000 hectares) pastoral property on the Cape River.

The party turned northward and passed close by the present-day site of Charters Towers to again reach the Burdekin River.

Opening up country

Here they were in the country of the Warungu people.

Allingham marked out his run, *Hillgrove*, with a site near the Basalt River for his homestead. Edward Cunningham chose his run on the eastern side of the Burdekin, 140,000 acres (56,655 hectares), which he named *Burdekin Downs*. Michael Miles, another member of the party, choose the adjoining *Fanning Downs*.

By 28 June 1861 they were back in Bowen to register their claim over the lands they had marked out for themselves with the Land Commissioner.

By now others were making their claims far to the west and to the north of Bowen.

"What happened on the Queensland frontier was part of a widespread campaign of frontier violence'."

Jonathan Richards

Chapter 3 - Frontier Violence

Most of the pioneer British settlers moving onto the pastoral properties to the west and north of Bowen that they had secured for themselves followed a policy of keeping the First Nations inhabitants out from their lands.

They forced them away from the river valleys and out from the other sources of water that the British wanted secure for their sheep and cattle.

They relied on the Queensland Native Mounted Police. This paramilitary force had accompanied Dalrymple to Bowen and along the way, they "dispersed" hundreds of First Nations people whose ancestors had occupied these lands and river valleys for centuries.

"Dispersing" was a euphemism. It meant the Queensland Native Police were responsible for the systematic killing of First Nations people. In Queensland, the policy of the British settlers was to wreak the most terrible revenge possible on the First Nation people [3].

What happened on the Queensland frontier was part of a "widespread campaign of frontier violence" [4].

In Queensland, New South Wales and Victoria colonial authorities used armed Indigenous forces for colonisation purposes just as they did in other parts of the British Empire.

The role of the Native Police was to protect the British land owners, the gold miners and settlers on the frontier.

In those first few years, conflict between settlers taking over the territory and the traditional owners throughout what the Queensland government had named the 'Kennedy District' was intense.

By 1863 almost the whole of the Kennedy District had been occupied by the British. In the next year, more land in the Cook and Bourke Districts was taken up.

---

[3] Evans, Raymond, Saunders, K. & Cronin, K. (1988) *Race Relations in Colonial Queensland.* St. Lucia, University of Qld Press, p.50

[4] Richards, Jonathan (2008) *The Secret War: a True History of Queensland's Native Police.* Brisbane, University of Queensland Press, p.4

> **In Queensland, New South Wales and Victoria colonial authorities used armed Indigenous forces for colonisation purposes just as they did in other parts of the British Empire.**

Pioneer pastoralist and historian, Edward Palmer, was one of the earliest to take up a run on the Cloncurry River which he called *Canobie*.

Ernest Henry, also in 1864, took up his run, *Hughenden* Station, on the Flinders River.

Pressure on the local First Nations people in these newly acquired pastoral districts intensified.

Native Police

By December 1861 Lieutenant Powell with his Native Mounted Police force cleared the Bogie River of First Nations people. On the Bowen River Powell's force had attacked groups of between sixty and eighty First Nations men, but many more remained.

More Native Mounted Police arrived in the Kennedy District in 1863, bringing the force's strength to twenty-three.

Seven of the newly arrived troopers promptly deserted. They joined local First Nations groups much to the consternation of the new settlers.

The settlers themselves and the police force sent to protect them were greatly outnumbered by the local inhabitants.

Fight for survival

First Nations people were soon aware that they were faced with a fight for survival. They were being driven off the Country that their families had nurtured and relied on forever.

They could no longer hunt and gather the food nor drink the water on which they and their children survived.

They were being hunted in their own lands.

Loos[5] quotes a correspondent writing in the *Port Denison Times* in November 1869 who explains what the policy of 'keeping the Aborigines out' entailed. It meant,

> "...never to allow them near a camp, out-station, head-station or township; consequently, they were to be hunted by anyone if seen in open country and driven away or shot down when caught out of the scrub and broken ground."

The effects of this policy meant the newcomers had to take the law into their own hands in self-defence. First Nations people retaliated and it became a scene of murder as well as the killing of sheep, cattle and horses.

This was an era of violent conflict in the Kennedy and neighbouring pastoral Districts. This

---

[5] Loos (1982) *Invasion and Resistance*. Canberra, Australian National University, p. 33.

continued so long as the policy of keeping them out was in force.

Pastoralists who did not follow the policy were able to establish good relationships with First Nations people in their area.

This process seems to have begun around 1868 when First Nations were admitted at *Natal Downs* on the Cape River and then at *Vane Creek* station on the Belyando River.

From around this time, the more intense conflict between the newcomers and First Nations people lessened, except on the very fringes of the areas of settlement.

There were still isolated attacks by First Nations people right up to the 1890s, but there were nowhere near the number of attacks and deaths on both sides as there had been between 1861 and 1870.

Loos[6] estimates that some 76 people died in that period from attacks by First Nations people. No accurate figure for First Nations deaths can be given, but a ratio of ten deaths for every one

---

[6] Loos (1982) p.193

person killed by them is considered very conservative.

"It was common for First Nations boys and girls to be taken as servants on pastoral properties all across Australia."

Marji Hill

Chapter 4 - The Mosmans

Jupiter Mosman, the First Nations boy who found the gold nugget at Charters Towers in 1871, got his Anglicised name from his boss, Hugh Mosman. We don't know about his First Nations name.

Archibald Mosman

Hugh Mosman (1843-1909), the gold prospector, was the eldest son of Archibald Mosman (1799-1863). Archibald at the age of 29 migrated to Sydney from Scotland in 1828 [7].

He opened a business in Sydney with his twin brother. This was a warehouse in George Street, Sydney from where they sent wool to their wool store in Liverpool, England.

---

[7] Stephen, M. D. "Mosman, Archibald (1799–1863)" in *Australian Dictionary of Biography*
https://adb.anu.edu.au/biography/mosman-archibald-2485

On the foreshores of Great Sirius Cove, which is now known as Mosman Bay on Sydney's North Shore, the Mosman brothers got a small land grant.

In 1832 they sold their warehouse and then at Great Sirius Cove they set up a whaling depot.

Mosman now owned most of the land which today is the Sydney suburb of Mosman. By 1835 Mosman had two whaling ships, the *Jane* and the *Tigress*, and he owned a third ship which traded with New Zealand.

In 1838 Mosman sold his shipping interests at Great Sirius Cove.

He purchased a sheep station called *Furracabad* in northern New South Wales. This was around 1845.

Mosman ultimately subdivided the property and it was here that the township of Glen Innes emerged.

Archibald Mosman eventually retired to Randwick in Sydney where he died in 1863. He and his wife, Harriet Farquharson, whom he married in 1847, were survived by ten children.

Hugh Mosman

Hugh Mosman, born at Mosman Bay in Sydney, was the eldest of these children. He was educated at Kings School in Parramatta.

Having lived on his father's property, Hugh Mosman had had some experience of life as a pastoralist in the Australian outback. In 1860 he travelled to Queensland to take up property in the newly opened north central areas of that colony.

His brother, Adam, and John Fraser were co-owners of the property, called *Tarbrax*.

In 1866 an international money crisis caused a collapse of the beef and wool markets. In Queensland, those pastoralists on stations far from settlements were the worst affected.

Hugh Mosman[8] like other young men had been attracted to Queensland in 1860 by the pastoral boom. However, suffering financially after the slump of 1866 he turned to prospecting.

The Mosman brothers and Fraser had held on as long as they could, but in 1871 they sold up and

---

[8] Bolton, G.C. "Mosman, Hugh (1843–1909)" in *Australian Dictionary of Biography* https://adb.anu.edu.au/biography/mosman-hugh-4261

Hugh Mosman and Fraser went prospecting for gold.

Jupiter Mosman

Hugh Mosman had taken a young First Nations boy that he saw at *Kynuna Station* as his servant or "horse boy". The boy had such large, luminous eyes that Mosman decided to call him Jupiter after the Greek god.

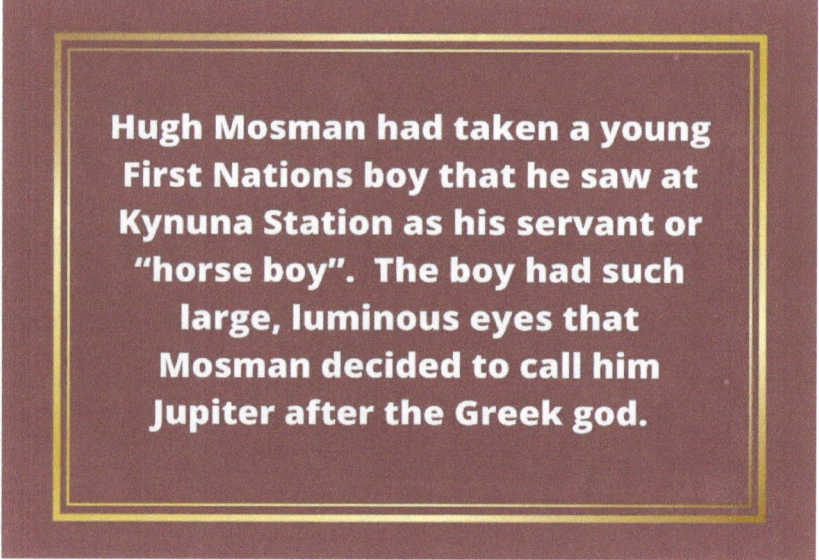

At that time Mosman and his brother Adam and their friend John Fraser owned the *Tarbrax*

property. *Kynuna* station lay about halfway between Winton and Cloncurry in Queensland. *Tarbrax* station was southwest, south of the Flinders River and towards the headwaters of the Diamantina River.

The First Nations people of the country where *Kynuna* was situated were the Wanamara. West of them was the Kalkadoon.

Jupiter could have been either Wanamara or Kalkadoon.

Servants

It was common for First Nations boys and girls to be taken as servants on pastoral properties all across Australia.

The Duracks, the great pastoralists of this era in the Kimberleys, had young First Nations boys between the ages of eight and fourteen working for them. This was happening within a few months of the Durack's arrival in the Kimberleys.

How these boys came to be servants of the Duracks and their team of overlanders is not known.

It is evident that some of these children were brought into the cattle stations after their parents had been killed in dispersal raids on their camps. Others were acquired in exchange for food, whilst still others were simply stolen from their families.

The editor of the *Port Denison Times* in 1869 reported overhearing a man say that he was going down to the First Nations camp at Queen's Beach to catch a young one.

In 1870 graziers, also known as "squatters", rode into the fringe camp on the Townsville common and took at least three children away. They finished up on properties as far away as Hughenden.

It was not unusual, too, for these children to be passed on from one owner to another.

A First Nations boy who had been a servant to Edward Palmer on *Canobie s*tation was passed on by Palmer's widow, as a sixteen-year-old, to a new owner in Brisbane.

Stolen Generations

There were probably a number of young First Nations boys on *Kynuna* when Mosman asked for and was given Jupiter. This was sometime in the late 1860s.

Gold! Hidden Stories of Australia's Past, Book 4

By 1871 the Mosman brothers and Fraser had sold *Tarbrax* to the owners of *Mount Emu* station. They headed to the goldfield at Ravenswood.

Jupiter went with them.

"Some surface gold was found. The richest discoveries, however, were the reefs of gold appearing as rocky outcrops on the surface."

Marji Hill

Chapter 5 - Gold

In the Kennedy District following the time the settlers took over their pastoral runs in North Queensland, neither the sheep nor the cattle industry flourished in those first few years.

The country was not suitable for sheep and though cattle did well, there was no market for beef apart from the few town dwellers in Bowen, Mackay and Townsville. Most of the cattle went to the boiling down works to produce tallow.

In 1866 a Reward Committee of leading pastoralists offered a prize of 1,000 pounds to anyone who discovered gold. The goldfield needed to yield at least 5,000 ounces of gold in a year, within 100 miles (nearly 161 kilometres) from Townsville.

Gold had already been found on the Star River, just over 112 kilometres from Townsville. Within three months it produced about 1,000 ounces of gold, but soon after the reef petered out.

Gold discoveries occurred on the Cape River and at Cloncurry in 1867 and on the Gilbert River in 1869.

Thousands of miners made their way to the new goldfields mostly looking for alluvial gold. This was found in soil deposited by rivers and creeks or in the river beds. It could be lying on the surface or a few metres underground.

When this surface gold was worked out miners tended to move on to other new gold discoveries. Some, however, were prepared to dig deeper into the gold-bearing quartz deposits and to follow the reefs down into the rock.

There were two cattle stations on the eastern side of the Burdekin River called *Ravenswood* and *Merri Merriwah*. A number of creek beds and gullies ran through these properties. In one of them, *Ravenswood* Station, a stockman, Thomas Aitken, found gold in 1868.

Prospectors were soon searching the creek beds and gold was discovered in several of them.

Some surface gold was found. The richest discoveries, however, were the reefs of gold appearing as rocky outcrops on the surface.

Gold! Hidden Stories of Australia s Past, Book 4

To work this gold rock crushing mills had to be transported to the mines by bullock wagons.

By the end of 1870, there were fifty-two mills at Ravenswood stamping the rock full time. Each ton of rock was expected to produce around 10 ounces of gold.

By this time hundreds of people were on the goldfield. The Gold Commissioner and Police Magistrate on the goldfield was W.S.E.M. Charters. His Clerk of Petty Sessions was W.R.O. Hill.

Hill[9] was later to write about his experiences of life on the Ravenswood field in his *Forty-five Years Experience in North Queensland*.

In all, the Ravenswood goldfield produced almost a million ounces of gold.

On to the Tors

Hugh Mosman, John Fraser and Jupiter Mosman arrived on the Ravenswood goldfield soon after the sale of *Tarbrax* Station.

---

[9] Hill, W.R.O. (1907) *Forty-five years Experience in North Queensland*. Brisbane: H.Pole.

At that time they would have known little, if anything, about prospecting for gold.

It was fortunate for them they were able to establish a friendship with a much-travelled and experienced prospector, George Clarke. Together with Clarke they set out heading first to the Broughton River diggings across the Burdekin and then turning northwest towards Sandy Creek.

It was late 1871.

George Clarke was to tell his version of the discovery of gold at Charters Towers some 20 years later to the editor of the *North Queensland Register*.

The three prospectors, Mosman, Fraser, and Clarke together with Jupiter Mosman fossicked the valleys of the Burdekin to the west and the north west. They found a little gold in the branches of the Broughton River and further towards the hills known as the Seventy Mile pinnacles.

The party were just over 100 kilometres from Ravenswood, around the area where Mount Leyshon is now. They had spent several weeks prospecting around the Seventy Mile area, mostly to the south and west. There were traces of gold, but not enough to excite them.

To the north, they could see what Clarke described as "a cluster of conical and square topped hills". These features of the landscape were to remind those from England of the English Tors.

Several kilometres from the Tors they found gold at a place Clarke calls the Merrie Monarch.

At this point, they were crossing the *Oregon* and *Texas* pastoral runs, which had been taken up on the traditional lands of the Gudjal people in 1863.

The gold prospectors had left the nearest water about eight kilometres behind them. They were in the dry country and they had to decide whether to press on or to go back to the water. A storm was threatening so they decided to press on to find a place to camp before it hit.

That was when a clap of thunder sent their pack horse galloping off into the bush with all their cooking gear. Soon rain began to fall heavily and they hastened to make camp.

It was 23 December, 1871.

"It was evident from the very beginning that this goldfield was not one that was going to peter out."

Marji Hill

Chapter 6 - The "World"

Christmas 1871 must have been a very exciting time for the three prospectors and Jupiter. They quickly found outcrops of gold-bearing rock that indicated the reefs below them.

The prospectors found surface gold like the nugget that Jupiter had found. However, it was the rich reefs that caught their imagination and got their attention.

Registering the gold claims

They marked out their claims on the best of the reefs that they found. Then Hugh Mosman rode to Ravenswood to register their claims with the Gold Commissioner.

Hugh Mosman would have ridden the 150 kilometres back to Ravenswood. That would have taken him probably a couple of days. Very likely Jupiter would have gone with him - after all, he was Hugh Mosman's boy, and not to be left with the other men.

The claim was registered on 2 January 1872. Almost two months later the new goldfield of Charters Towers was officially proclaimed on 26 February.

The new goldfield

By that date, the gold rush had started. Between four and five hundred people were on the field and over 100 claims had been pegged out.

Writing from Ravenswood to the *Port Denison Times*[10] on 24 February, a correspondent reported that Ravenswood would suffer because so many diggers were leaving to go to the new field at Charters Towers. The feeling was that the new gold rush would eclipse anything else known in Queensland.

There were many reefs. Two that were pegged by Mosman, Clarke and Fraser, the North Australian and General Wyndham, proved to be among the richest on the Charters Towers goldfield.

---

[10] Pike G. (1996) *Queensland frontier.* 3rd ed. Brisbane: G.Pike.p. 234

The reefs lay in fissures between hard granite. They went deep underground. The miners had to go many thousands of feet under the surface. Soon only mines owned by companies of shareholders and employing miners would occupy the field.

It was evident from the very beginning that this goldfield was not one that was going to peter out.

A town was set up; merchants had to supply the needs of the miners and banks were established.

Initially, the township was laid out at Millchester but later it shifted to its present site.

Young Jupiter would have been there in the midst of the excitement of those early days of gold discovery. In those first few weeks on each new day, new miners came onto the field. They were keen to stake out a claim. Tents were pitched and miners were alert to any rumour of a new strike.

Jupiter would have been there watching. He must have wondered at the gold fever - the excitement for those rocks that shimmered in the sunlight, and the grey stone with its tiny flecks of gold.

There would be few who would have known, or wanted to know, his version of how the gold was discovered.

Clarke, Fraser and Mosman were the official discoverers of gold at Charters Towers. If they noticed Jupiter at all it was only to dismiss him as Mosman's horse boy.

Early Charters Towers goldfield

Charters Towers

The First Nations people of the gold town that became Charters Towers are called Gudjal (pronounced Goodjal). The Gudjal lived along the Burdekin and Broughton Rivers around the basalt country[11]. The Gudjal shared their boundaries to the north with the Gugu Badhun with whom they had strong ceremonial and kinship ties.

Gudjal Language

The Gudjal language was spoken by First Nations people from the Charters Towers region of North Queensland [12].

In the late 1850s and 1860s, the Gudjal were the traditional custodians of the land that was taken over by those seeking their property empires for cattle and sheep and those wanting to make their fortunes mining for gold.

As happened all over the Queensland frontier the local First Nations people resisted the taking over of their traditional lands. North west of Charters Towers around the Basalt Wall

---

[11] Babidge, Sally Marie (2007) *Written True, Not Gammon! A History of Aboriginal Charters Towers.* Thuringowa, Qld: Black Ink Press, p.1
[12] Santo, W. *Gudjal Language Pocket Dictionary.* Black Ink Press, 2006

resistance took the form of spearing livestock and threatening the lives of the new settlers.

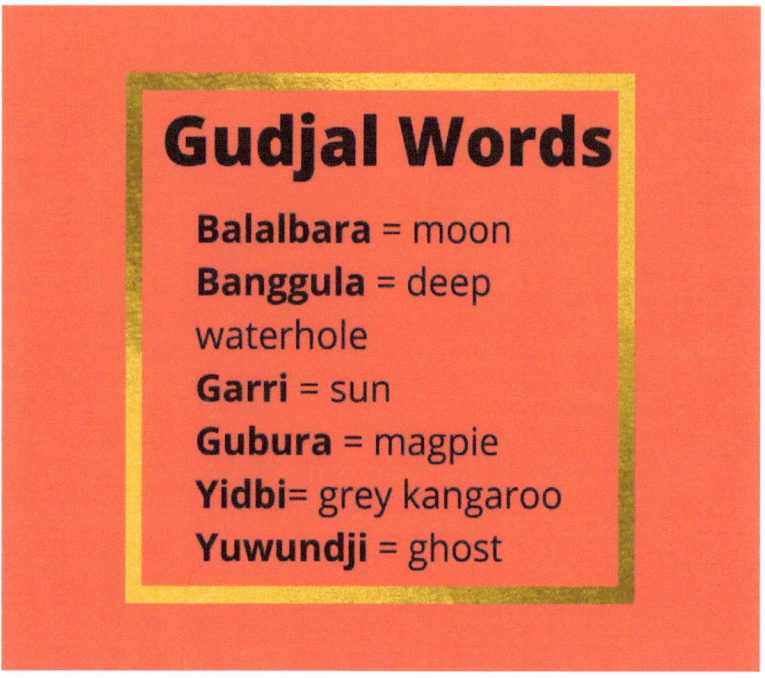

Gudjal Words

Balalbara = moon
Banggula = deep waterhole
Garri = sun
Gubura = magpie
Yidbi = grey kangaroo
Yuwundji = ghost

Babidge[13] reports how in 1858 the Commandant of the Native Police for Queensland instructed his men that it was their duty 'at all times and opportunities to disperse large assemblages of blacks'.

---

[13] Babidge, Sally Marie, p.3

Native Mounted Police were employed in the Charters Towers goldfield, the black troopers being utilised because of their ability to track people in the bush. Europeans on mining and pastoral settlements feared attacks from First Nations people.

Oral histories from local First Nations people point to stories of killings and massacres which were part of the dispossession process. It was a brutal outcome of the early history of contact between the new Europeans and the traditional owners of the country.

Town Life

Gudjal people were always part of the town life of Millchester and Charters Towers. First Nations camps were established around Charters Towers and Millchester and at places such as Sandy Creek, Sheep Station Creek, out at the Broughton River, and at the Burdekin Pumping Station.

Traditional ceremonies were held with men and women painted with their clan designs and the women beating time with their digging sticks. Gudjal people hunted larger animals for meat and collected bush tucker and European tea, sugar, flour and tobacco also became popular for those living close to town.

There is no evidence of First Nations people ever having been involved in the mining for gold in this region apart from the fact that it was Jupiter Mosman who actually made the discovery of gold.

Babidge[14] says some First Nations men were employed to cut bark sheets for the new settlers in the town with which they built their houses. Others got an income as yardmen for hotels, in dairies, carting wood for the mines or working at the Burdekin Pumping Station.

Many First Nations people lived in the countryside around Charters Towers. At certain times of the year, they came into the town. One of these occasions was 'Blanket Day', when blankets were handed out by the Government at the Charters Towers Court House.

They also received government rations of tea, flour, sugar and tobacco. This was the Protection era when the government authorities thought the First Nations were a dying race because of

---

[14] Babidge, Sally Marie, p. 9

the killings, introduced diseases, sickness and loss of land and natural resources.

There were the First Nations people who came to Charters Towers from other areas. They may have been brought there by force or coerced by police, pastoralists, prospectors and explorers.

Jupiter Mosman, who found the first gold nugget in Charters Towers at Christmas 1871, was not a local to Charters Towers.

After the discovery of gold, the mining town of Charters Towers grew. There were miners, butchers, bakers, grog sellers, the bullockies with their wagons, police, bankers and all the other government officials needed to control a mining town.

There were arguments over mining leases, robberies, drunken squabbles, accidents and murders.

Riot

A riot erupted late in that first year when a butcher, Trevethan, raised the price of beef from four pence to six pence a pound.

Hill[15] who was Clerk of Petty Sessions at Ravenswood at the time, provided a personal account of the events that followed.

There were those miners who were unlucky on the goldfield. The alluvial gold quickly petered out. The small amount of gold some of them had found as they fossicked the arid gullies was barely sufficient to pay for their daily needs.

On a Saturday night in early November of 1872 a mob of about 800 miners, probably drunk gathered around Trevethan's butcher shop in the Millchester camp.

They tied a long rope around the gable of the shop and pulled it off its foundations out onto the dirt road. Three of the ringleaders were arrested and locked up in the Charters Towers lockup.

The group now armed itself and set off to the lockup demanding that the prisoners be released. They were persuaded to remain calm and the prisoners were released on bail.

---

[15] Hill, W.R.O. (1907) *Forty-five years Experience in North Queensland.* Brisbane: H.Pole, pp.57-58

Hill had received orders to head for Charters Towers from his office in Ravenswood and to take as many police with him as could be mustered.

He found five.

The following day and night the protesters were still stirred up. Again, they had had too much alcohol since they forced the grog shops to remain open throughout the Sunday.

The Court was held on Monday morning in one of the grog shops, and Trevethan rode in on his horse to give evidence against the three men.

The protesters rushed him as he was dismounting, but an Inspector of police, Trevethan's brother and Hill himself with some others, prevented them from killing him on the spot.

They hurled bottles and stones at him as he was being escorted into the temporary court. Trevethan drew his revolver and fired into the crowd. He wounded two of his assailants.

The mob was ready to lynch him on the spot. They did manage to belt him up before he could be got away and bundled-into Court.

The Catholic Bishop, Quinn, then harangued the crowd and managed to calm them long enough for the police to get Trevethan away by horse under escort to Ravenswood.

The protesters wrecked the lockup looking for Trevethan and continued to riot through the night. Extra police were moved into Charters Towers over the next few days. Other ringleaders of the riot were arrested and punished.

Trevethan was not tried for shooting his assailants, given that only one of them was seriously wounded but recovered.

Trevethan was not seen again in Charters Towers.

Did Jupiter witness the riots over that dramatic weekend? Probably.

Successful miners

Mosman and his partners were successful miners. They had pegged three of the rocky gold-bearing outcrops that would lead to three of the richest long-working reefs in the Charters Towers goldfield.

Surface quartz on one of their reefs, the Washington, produced 1,600 ounces of gold alone. They did not need to do much digging to pile up heaps of gold-bearing stone.

The first two gold escorts out of Charters Towers in that first year took away 60,000 ounces of gold. A fair proportion of that could well have come from Mosman's and his partners 'mines.

Between 1872 and 1886 Mosman is reported to have floated or to have invested in several of the companies formed to exploit the deep reefs.

They had no need to attack a poor butcher for raising the prices of his beef!

Bustling mining town

To really mine the reefs once the surface stone had been dug down a few feet, machinery had to be installed to sink the shafts deep down through the rock. They had to crush the gold-bearing stone as it was brought to the surface.

Charters Towers in that first year of 1872 was a busy, bustling place. Wagons hauled the quartz stone to the crushers along dusty, pot-holed, dirt tracks.

The stampers clanged unceasingly as they crushed the rock. Timber getters were out cutting the firewood for the crushers and hauling it back to the town.

Soon sawmills were at work preparing the timber to line the shafts as the mines went deeper down after the reefs.

Government offices and the courts were busy, recording claims, issuing licences, and settling disputes.

Make-shift shops lined the tracks that were to become the main streets of the town, offering their wares to the women and children and to the miners and others as they paraded up and down looking for what they could afford.

By the end of 1872, the population between Millchester and Charters Towers was over 3,000 people.

Once the alluvial and easily dug surface gold had been mined many of the miners headed off to other finds, unwilling to stay as waged miners digging out other people's gold.

But others took their place so that by 1892, 20,000 people lived and worked in Charters Towers. The town became the second city of

Queensland and the capital in the north of the Colony.

> **By 1892, 20,000 people lived and worked in Charters Towers. The town became the second city of Queensland, and capital in the north of the Colony.**

People called it "The World".

By that time, too, the gold mines had yielded nearly 2,300,000 ounces of gold valued at 8,000,000 pounds sterling.

"...Jupiter went droving."

Marji Hill

Chapter 7 - Away from the Golden Frenzy

The length of time that Jupiter remained in Charters Towers is not known.

Schooling

One of the early pioneers in Charters Towers thought that Hugh Mosman had sent Jupiter to school at Newtown in Sydney and later at Lyndhurst College where he was baptised as a Roman Catholic and given the names John Joseph. This was a Catholic boarding school for boys run by the Benedictine Order at Glebe.

Jupiter rejoined Mosman in Charters Towers during vacations, playing football and cricket in local teams. Under Mosman's enthusiastic tutelage he became an excellent horseman.

Jupiter accompanied Mosman on his visits to Sydney but, when Hugh Mosman accepted the nomination to the Queensland Legislative Council, he and Jupiter finally parted.

Lyndhurst was closed down in the mid-1870s, and no records exist in the Sydney diocesan registers for that period of a Baptism of any John Joseph Mosman. Nor has the diocesan archives any of the school records.

Mark Warren[16], writing in the *Northern Miner* in 1996, says that in a eulogy read at a ceremony held at Jupiter's new grave site in the Charters Towers cemetery, it was claimed that Jupiter in his years of retirement often spoke to a Catholic religious Sister who had befriended him about his years in Lyndhurst.

Jupiter is also said to have told the Sister that he had been baptised.

It is unlikely that Jupiter would have had any education before becoming Hugh Mosman's personal horse boy. There would have been no time for schooling in those early years. At the age of eleven or twelve formal schooling, would have been impossible.

---

1. [16] Warren, Mark (1996) *Northern Miner* 6 December, p.5

To have sent a young First Nations boy with no former schooling, and who was used to daily life in the saddle in the harsh Queensland bush, to a boarding school run by religious monks far away in Sydney would have been the grossest cruelty.

Given the available evidence, it is more likely that Jupiter stayed with Hugh Mosman in Charters Towers until he was ready to go droving.

However, the question of Jupiter's schooling remains open. If he did study at Lyndhurst for a while, it was not really any advantage to him.

A policeman[17] in Charters Towers in 1917 said that Jupiter had minimal schooling. All he could do was sign his name and read small words.

Horse racing

Horse racing was one of Hugh Mosman's passions. He was to pursue it throughout his lifetime, and in 1902 he won the Queensland Turf Club Derby in Brisbane.

The Charters Towers Jockey Club was formed almost as soon as the goldfield was proclaimed.

---

[17] Andrews, T (1917) Acting Sergeant, Charters Towers. Letter

It became the headquarters of racing in North Queensland with meetings being held every few weeks.

According to Marsland[18] racing was always enjoyed in the new town of Charters Towers with a strict racing committee and supervision of the whole operation. Every effort went into ensuring that the racing was run honestly.

The races always attracted great crowds and the horses that raced were very well-bred.

Given that Hugh Mosman's discovery of gold had made him one of the wealthy miners in the town, and given his passion for horse racing, it is very possible that he was one of the founders of the Jockey Club and had horses racing at the Club's meetings.

There would have been a role for Jupiter there, caring for Hugh Mosman's horses.

Hugh Mosman had his left forearm blown off one day in 1882 when a stick of dynamite went off in his hand. He had been fishing with the dynamite.

---

[18] Marsland, L.W. (1892) The Charters Towers Gold Mines. London: Waterlow Bros., p.5

He did recover and continued to be highly respected socially in Charters Towers. His two sisters, Cecilia and Harriette, had each married prominent Queensland politicians. Cecilia was married to Sir Arthur Palmer, and Harriette was Sir Thomas MacIlwraith's second wife.

In 1891 Hugh Mosman was nominated to the Queensland Legislative Council, sometimes called the 'Squatters House', and he remained there till he resigned in 1905.

Hugh Mosman died in Brisbane in 1909. His estate was valued then at 70,000 pounds sterling. Hugh Mosman never married and, when he died his considerable fortune was divided between his nephews and nieces. Jupiter was not mentioned in the will.

When Jupiter finally parted from High Mosman, Jupiter went droving.

"By the 1890s white stockmen recognised the mustering abilities of First Nations stockmen, the European ones never quite reaching that same standard."

Marji Hill

Chapter 8 - Droving Days

Jupiter probably stayed with Hugh Mosman until he departed the town to take up his nomination to the Queensland Legislative Council. If that is so, Jupiter would have been around thirty years old when he went droving.

A nephew of Hugh Mosman, possibly his brother Adam's son, was to overland a large herd of cattle from near *Kynuna* to Wodonga in Victoria. He invited Jupiter to join the drive, and with his long-term 'boss' leaving, Jupiter was happy to accept.

The drive was very successful taking them just over six months.

Epic overland cattle drives

Driving cattle hundreds and thousands of kilometres across the country was the only way in those years that cattlemen could get cattle onto distant station properties or get them from their properties to the best markets.

> **Driving cattle hundreds and thousands of kilometres across the country was the only way in those years that cattlemen could get cattle onto distant station properties, or get them from their properties to the best markets.**

A comprehensive, detailed and very rich history of Australia's stockmen, and their work in the cattle industry is given by Glen McLaren in his book *Big Mobs: the Story of Australian Cattlemen* [19].

Oscar De Satge, who took up *Peak Downs* to the northeast of Clermont in Queensland in 1861, as a young man drove cattle from the Darling

---

[19] McLaren, Glen (2000) *Big Mobs: the Story of Australian Cattlemen.* Fremantle: Fremantle Arts Centre, p.53

Downs to Brisbane with a couple of young First Nations men to help him.

In 1860 Christopher Allingham had driven a herd of 8,000 sheep and 2,000 cattle from Armidale in New South Wales to the Don River near Bowen in Queensland. That drive took just over six months.

A Victorian, Thomas Hamilton, with only two men to assist him, one of them a First Nations man, drove his stock from his family property in Victoria over 3,000 kilometres north to Darwin in 1871. His drive took nearly two years.

Two drives in 1883 capped them all.

Charles MacDonald and the McKenzie brothers drove their herd 5,632 kilometres from just near Goulburn in NSW to the junction of the Margaret and Fitzroy Rivers in the Kimberleys in Western Australia. It took them three years, through Coopers Creek to the headwaters of the Diamantina, then west across the MacDonnell Ranges and on to the Kimberleys.

Not one head of their original herd survived the drive but they had enough cattle to found one of the great Australian cattle empires on their *Fossil Downs* station.

The other great overland drive of that year was that by the Duracks who, with twenty-five men, herded 7,250 cattle, 200 horses and 60 bullocks from *Thylungra* station in Queensland to the Ord River in the Kimberleys in just over two years.

These were some of the epic journeys overland. Droving their cattle long distances to the best markets was what the cattlemen expected to have to do.

The best markets lay in the southern colonies where the cities were growing rapidly and with them the market for beef and lamb.

In 1880 the first shipment of chilled meat from Australia was successfully unloaded in London from the *S.S. Strathleven*. By the turn of the century, more than a million beef and sheep carcases were being shipped to Britain from the chilled meat processing plants in the south of Australia.

The best beef cattle at that time came from the new cattle properties in the centre and north of Queensland. What was important in exploiting these chilled meat markets was to get the cattle to the processing plants in the best possible condition.

Therein lay the skill of the drover.

By the 1890s white stockmen recognised the mustering abilities of First Nations stockmen, the European ones never quite reaching that same standard [20].

Not only did First Nations stockmen prove to be superb horsemen, they knew the bush and they had unequalled skill as trackers. All of these were qualities needed both for mustering the herds and culling them for the market and then for overlanding them.

Work of the stockmen

When Jupiter joined Hugh Mosman's nephew at *Kynuna*, the work of mustering, drafting and culling the herd for overlanding was about to begin.

Mustering meant long hours in the saddle and out in the bush rounding up the wild cattle and driving them into the holding yards. This was where First Nations' stockmen like Jupiter came into their own.

---

[20] McLaren, Glen, *ibid,* p.53

Not all the cattle roamed the plains in large tame herds that could be easily driven together and headed towards the yards. Rather there would be a number of wild cattle off in small mobs, up the gullies, round the waterholes, down in the creek beds and out in the scrub. There were bulls, there were heifers, there were bullocks, there were cows and there were calves.

The cattle had to be brought out into the open, herded together, calmed down, prevented from splitting away and driven to the yards. Mustering could take days of hard riding.

There was nearly always at least one beast that would try to break away from the rest, that had to be run down, turned and herded back to the others. Galloping through scrub after a bullock that had split from the mob was a hazardous exercise calling for a sure-footed horse, supreme riding skills and sharp eyesight.

Often a number of station owners with their stockmen would come together to muster. Together they would drive the wild cattle and unbranded calves out into the open, join them to the tame herds and head them to the stockyards.

As the herds were moving, stockmen would parole the flanks ready to cut off any beast that tried to break away and wheel it back into the herd.

Once locked away in the stockyards the herd had to be drafted. The cattle were moved from the holding paddocks and stockyards into the drafting yards. One yard held the unbranded calves, a second the breeding or store stock, and the third the bullocks.

As the cattle were driven through the pens the station bosses and their most experienced stockmen manned the drafting gates leading into the yards. At the shout, "Calf!", or "Store!", or "Bush!", one or other gate was opened and the animal chased through it.

All the unbranded cattle, calves and any others which had previously escaped the muster, would be branded and the male calves castrated.

If bullocks were to be sent overland to the markets, now was the time to cut them out from the yards. The muster might have brought in several thousand beasts.

After the muster, there could have been two to three thousand bullocks. The station bosses would have culled their own bullocks from the main herd.

It now remained for them to select the fittest and fattest of the bullocks, cut them out from the mass of other bullocks and herd them together to start their journey.

This was not as easy to do as it may sound. Stockmen had to ride into the middle of the herd and quietly move the chosen bullock to the outside, being careful not to allow it to turn back.

The bullocks cut out from the others had to be kept separate until they could be sent on their way. Experience had shown that the ideal mob for a long drive was around 1,500 head.

Cattle drive

Once the station owners had assembled their cattle they were handed over to the team of overlanders.

This is what would have happened at *Kynuna* when Hugh Mosman's nephew with Jupiter and the other members of their team began the drive to Wodonga.

We can only guess what Jupiter's role in the team was.

Hugh Mosman's nephew was the boss drover. There would have been a cook, six or more drovers and the horse tailer. This latter had the most important job of looking after the drover's horses and spare equipment and packs of supplies.

Each drover would have a string of horses, called a 'plant', resting some while he worked others, and using chosen horses with special skills as they were needed. Given that he had been Mosman's horse boy, there is every possibility that Jupiter took the job of horse tailer on the drive.

At the beginning of a drive, the cattle needed to be moved carefully away from the station. Usually, the station stockmen would accompany the drovers to do this, keeping the mob headed off the familiar station land and away from the sounds of the herds they were used to.

Once on the road, the drovers worked to keep the mob together, quickly heading off any bullock that tried to break away and working to settle them down into a routine.

Stock routes

By the time of this drive to Wodonga, drovers had learned a great deal about handling cattle in the Australian bush. Stock routes south and west had been mapped out and were regularly used.

In time, in Queensland and in the southern colonies, they were to be gazetted by their governments as reserved routes around and along the borders of the station properties along the way. From *Kynuna* the stock route to Wodonga headed south to where Winton is now, then on to Longreach, past Windorah, Thargomindah and on to Hungerford on the border of Queensland and New South Wales.

In New South Wales they headed for Bourke, Wilcannia, Hay, then down to the Murray River and on to Wodonga.

The boss drovers staged their drive so as to bring their cattle onto water around the middle of the day, and onto open grazing ground at the end of the day. They also had to bring the cattle to their market in the best possible condition.

The most direct route from *Kynuna* to Wodonga is about 2,000 kilometres.

The stock route followed in the 1890s was probably about 500 kilometres longer. Since the drive took the young Mosman and his team six months, allowing time along the way to rest up the cattle and to bring them on in the best possible condition, a daily stage could have been from fifteen to twenty kilometres.

The mob had to be watched through the night. The boss drover usually took the late watch, around 3.00 am. Then the men had to be up and ready to start the mob on its way at dawn.

The cook and the horse tailer were the first up. When breakfast was ready the cook would call the drovers. By that time the horse tailer would have brought in the horses and sorted out those the drovers had nominated as their mounts for the day.

Work of the drovers

After a hurried breakfast, the horses were saddled up and the drovers were ready to move the cattle on.

A couple would take up a position near to the front on either side of the cattle, another couple on either side at the rear and the rest between them covering the flanks of the mob on either side.

The drovers had to keep the beasts moving steadily on in the right direction, watching for breakaways, but not worrying too much about the stragglers who would come back to the herd when it was next rested.

The aim was to cover as much distance as possible in the morning before bringing the cattle onto the water. The boss drover's job was to scout ahead to find the best place to water the animals and then to move on to choose the campsite for the night.

This needed to be out in the open away from dense bush, with reasonable grazing and away from anything that might tend to spook the cattle in the night. Campsites and watering places would have been identified up to two or three days ahead.

Traditional droving could not have been done without horses. The cook and horse tailer had the job of breaking camp each morning, packing up and loading the packs on the packhorses. Then they would head off to the next designated campsite, set up and have food ready for the drovers when they came into camp.

The drovers would have moved the herd on from water in time to get them to the night camp. Once there the cattle were herded together and kept in tight to settle for the night.

One or more of the drovers would ride ahead of them in shifts throughout the night. Every drover had a horse that was particularly good for night work because of its ability to see in the dark and to avoid stumbling over fallen trees or tramping on dried sticks.

Unusual sounds in the night could frighten one or more beasts in the herd and start a rush among the rest. Drovers found that singing softly or gently humming could help keep the herd calm.

Mosman and his team must have been quick to control any rushes on the drive from *Kynuna* to Wodonga to have brought the mob safely, without loss, to market.

At the evening camps, the horse tailer[21] responsible for getting horses to water and feed would collect the horses as the drovers dismounted and removed their saddles and bridles. He would hobble them for the night so that they wouldn't stray too far and he would tether the night horses that the drovers would ride during their watch.

Early in the morning just before the sun rose, it was important for the horse tailer to be able to locate the horses quickly and to bring them into the camp and have them ready for the drovers when it was time to get the mob moving.

Jupiter was an experienced horse tracker and would have had no trouble finding any horses that may have strayed some distance in the night.

Jupiter would also have been skilled in the two other important tasks of the horse tailer. He had to make sure that the horses remained in good condition and that the loads on the pack horses were properly balanced and fastened firmly.

---

[21] McLaren, Glen, *ibid*, p.84

Gold! Hidden Stories of Australia's Past,
Book 4

"Up until 1965 if you were a First Nations worker in the pastoral industry you were paid less than white workers."

Marji Hill

Chapter 9 - Service to the Cattle Industry

Following the big drive to Wodonga, Jupiter Mosman worked as a drover on the cattle stations around Charters Towers. Two of those were *Lolworth* and *Dotswood*.

Cattle stations

Lolworth was southeast of Charters Towers. It was situated between the Cape River and one of its tributaries, Lolworth Creek. The entrance to the station now is from the Flinders Highway as it runs from Charters Towers to Hughenden.

Dotswood lies almost due north of Charters Towers, bordering on *Burdekin Downs*. Jupiter also worked at *Wambianna* and *Stockyard Creek* stations.

Dotswood was the pastoral property that was originally taken up by Phillip Somer. This was the man, who in 1861 with Edward Cunningham, had been attacked by a group of First Nations men and was knocked unconscious by a boomerang.

Somer had originally taken up a run on the Cape River whilst Cunningham took up *Burdekin Downs*. As was the custom of the times Somer put in a manager to run *Dotswood* for him.

The manager, Thornton, is remembered as the pioneer of a bullock team route from Townsville over the Herveys Range, through Thornton's Gap, across *Dotswood* and on to Dalrymple on the Burdekin.

The township of Dalrymple no longer exists but the roadway remains. Somers sold *Dotswood* in 1866 and, like Hugh Mosman did later, went mining.

Robert Towns[22], who recruited and exploited blackbirded South Sea Islanders, to work on his sugar cane farms in southern Queensland, became the part-owner of *Dotswood*. His partner was John Melton Black, who acted as Towns' agent in North Queensland.

---

[22] McKinnon, A. (2019) www.themonthly.com.au/issue/2019/july/1561989600/alex-mckinnon/blackbirds-australia-s-hidden-slave-trade-history

Jupiter worked on these cattle stations from the 1890s to his retirement in the 1930s. Throughout this time he was to see many changes.

The railway

There was the railway from Townsville to Charters Towers in 1882. It had taken five years to build that far. Two years later it had linked Ravenswood to Charters Towers before stretching on from Charters Towers to Hughenden. Eventually, it touched the edge of the Barkly Tableland beyond Cloncurry and Mt. Isa.

Meat

In 1884 the railway started carrying livestock between Townsville and Charters Towers. Whilst big cattle drives still happened well into the 1890s to the southern railheads at Bourke, Muswellbrook and Wodonga so that they could be sold on the Sydney and Melbourne markets, demand for beef at the meat works in Townsville was rapidly increasing.

By 1898 meat processing works in Townsville were taking over fifty thousand head of cattle a year.

By 1900 the Ross River freezing works were processing between twenty and thirty thousand a year.

There were other meat works at Sellheim and at Merinda, near Bowen. Between them, the meat works of North Queensland were processing over 40% of all the cattle being treated in the colony in 1898.

Some cattle were transported to the meat works by train. However, it was still cheaper for the pastoralists to overland their herds if they were close to the meat processing plants.

The increased demand for beef from the North Queensland properties did not mean that any great change took place in the working conditions and the cattle growing methods. Pastoralists did set about improving the quality of their herds but the routine of the cattle station life remained much the same year by year.

That routine was seasonal.

Mustering

Mustering took place at the end of summer. Stockmen would spend long hours in the saddle each day during mustering time.

Their job was to mind the herd and stopping the herd from splitting was the stockman's main task. He needed a good horse to be able to get quickly onto a stray and turn it back into the mob.

Jupiter is said to have ridden big chestnut horses bred from a famous sire called 'Collector'.

The stockman stayed with the herd day and night until mustering was over. Once they had settled down for the night, he could make his fire, boil the billy and eat his supper, before wrapping himself in his blanket to grab some rest.

Next day he would need to be up before dawn to bring in his horse, get breakfast and be ready to move with the herd when it stirred.

Some properties had two musters a year, but there were others that might have four musters.

The most hazardous of the stockman's jobs was rounding up the scrubbers – 'wild cattle that had escaped earlier musters and hid in the thick scrub'.

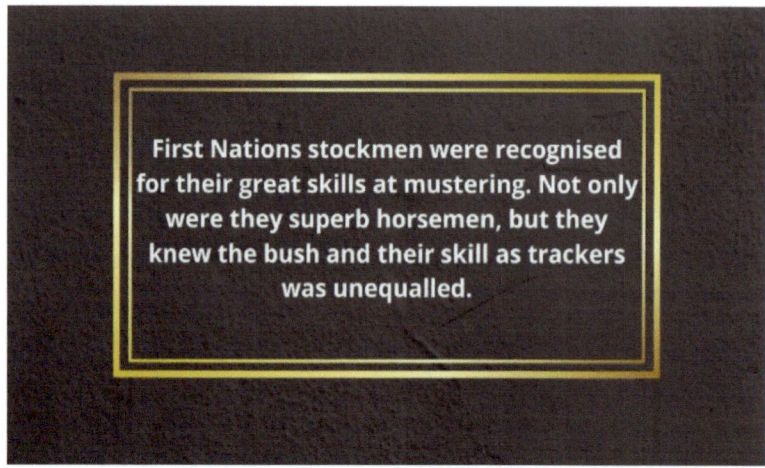

First Nations stockmen were recognised for their great skills at mustering. Not only were they superb horsemen, but they knew the bush and their skill as trackers was unequalled.

All of these qualities were needed both for mustering the herds, culling them for the market and then for overlanding them.

As a stockman working on *Lolworth* and *Dotswood* and other stations around Charters Towers, Jupiter Mosman would have done his share of mustering.

First Nations workers

Up until 1965 if you were a First Nations worker in the pastoral industry you were paid less than white workers.

In Queensland and the other colonies, up until the late 1890s and beyond, most First Nations workers on cattle stations depended on the generosity of the station managers and owners for their pay.

Generally, they were given only their keep – clothes, food, and tobacco. The equipment they used belonged to the station as did the horses they rode.

In some places, they were given credit at the station store where they could obtain some small luxuries.

The Act

With the passing in Queensland of the 1897 Aboriginals Protection and Restriction of the Sale of Opium Act and subsequent amendments, First Nations pastoral workers were given a minimum wage.

Initially, this was bitterly opposed. It was thought that by setting a minimum wage for First Nations workers would open the way for white workers to claim a minimum wage too.

At first, the minimum wage for First Nations workers in the pastoral industry was set at five shillings a month.

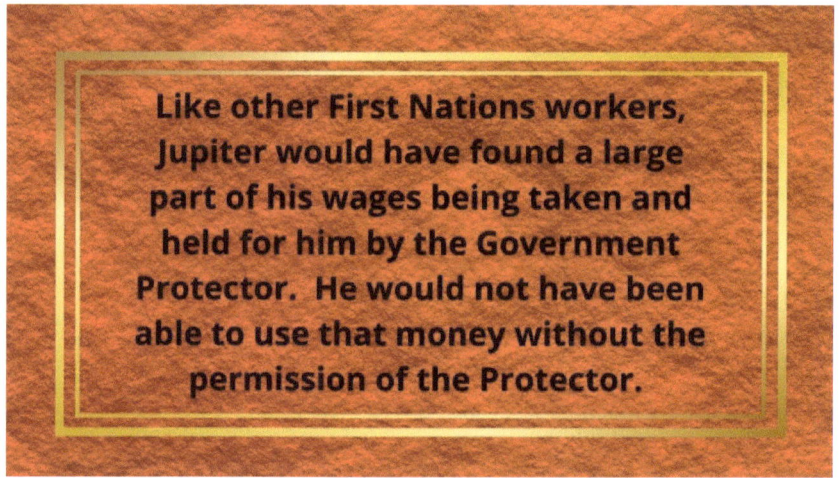

Like other First Nations workers, Jupiter would have found a large part of his wages being taken and held for him by the Government Protector. He would not have been able to use that money without the permission of the Protector.

In 1917 a Charters Towers solicitor, W.T. Mitchell, wrote to the Under Secretary of the Home Secretary's Department in Brisbane, requesting on Jupiter's behalf that he be exempted from that section of the 1897 Act which required that half of his drover's pay be paid to the Protector of Aborigines.

The request was rejected by the Chief Protector of Aborigines. This rejection was on the grounds that Jupiter being a First Nations person covered by definition in the Act was not entitled to the exemption.

The real reason for denying the exemption is revealed in a report[23] on Jupiter to the Chief Protector of Aborigines by the local Protector, Sub-Inspector of Police Ryan.

> *I have the honour to report,* he said, *that Jupiter Mosman (an Aboriginal) is an intelligent old man who has been with white people all his life.*
>
> *He is aware of the value of money and no doubt could manage his own affairs, but is addicted to drink – he has two convictions.*

---

[23] Ryan, W.A. (1917) Sub-Inspector, Protector of Aboriginals. Letter.

> *I attach the report by Acting Sergeant Andrews who knows the boy very well.*
>
> *For Jupiter's own protection I consider it is to his advantage to be left as he is.*

On the issue of having an alcohol addiction Andrews said that on those occasions when he did come to town, which would not have been frequent, Jupiter always had a quantity of cash.

He was able to get alcohol through his contacts in the white community. As a result, "in a half drunken state" he tended to "become very impudent"[24]. In the circumstances, it is clear why the Acting Sergeant and the Inspector of police were reluctant to allow this "impudent boy" access to the rest of the money that he had earned.

Discrimination

This inclination by the authorities to treat this "intelligent old man" as an unreliable "boy" was further evidenced in 1923 when M.J.Hogan[25], Superintendent of the Cairns Ambulance, sought

---

[24] Andrews, T, (1917) Acting Sergeant. Letter 1917
[25] Chief Protector of Aboriginals. Memorandum 4 August 1923.

permission from the Chief Protector to bring Jupiter to Cairns for the Golden Seventies Exhibition to commemorate the discoveries of gold in the 1870s.

By that time Jupiter was the only surviving member of the prospecting group which had first discovered gold in Charters Towers.

Jupiter was working on *Dotswood Station* under a Mr Real. Approval to be absent from work for the ten days of travel and attendance at the exhibition was given by Mr. Real.

The local Protector gave his approval and the Chief Protector informed Superintendent Hogan that the Department "had no objection to Jupiter Mosman going to Cairns" provided that the costs of his journey to Cairns were sent in advance to the protector in Charters Towers.

Presumably, on his return journey, Jupiter would be handed his ticket at the Cairns station and sent on his way.

No money for travel was to be trusted to Jupiter.

"A First Nations man, a prospector, a drover, and a man of dignity – that was Jupiter Mosman."

Marji Hill

Chapter 10 - A Man of Dignity

Jupiter Mosman died on 5 December 1945. He was buried in an unmarked grave.

Honouring Jupiter's memory

On the fiftieth anniversary of Jupiter's death, a large gathering from all sections of the Charters Towers community met at his graveside to honour his memory.

The gathering recognised Jupiter's contribution to the discovery of gold at Charters Towers, his long years of service to the cattle industry, and the statesman-like and diplomatic role he played in promoting goodwill among the varied groups of people living in Charters Towers.

Jupiter Mosman is commemorated in the Australian Prospectors and Miner's Hall of Fame in Kalgoorlie, Western Australia[26].

---

[26] Australian Prospectors & Miners Hall of Fame "Mosman, Jupiter" http://www.mininghalloffame.com.au/hall-of-fame/inductee.php?id=69

In Centenary Park across the road from Eventide Home in Charters Towers there is a statue of him finding that first gold nugget.

Jupiter Mosman

His portrait, painted by myself, hangs in the foyer of the World Theatre in Charters Towers.

For many years the large painting celebrating the discovery of gold by Jupiter Mosman and the rest of the prospecting team hung in the foyer of the former *Jupiters Casino* in Townsville.

The First Nations organisation set up in the 1970s was named the Jupiter Mosman Aboriginal Community Co-operative Society. *Jupiters Casino* on Queensland's Gold Coast and the casino in Townsville were named after him.

Although Jupiter Mosman himself was not from Charters Towers, he was still well respected and welcomed by the local First Nations community. He was made to share in their stories and their traditions.

The local Gudjal people's story was one that Jupiter's own people shared. It was the story that First Nations people across the Australian continent experienced.

When Jupiter finished with droving sometime in the early 1930s, he had his savings banked and was able to live on them in Charters Towers for a few years.

Old age

By 1936, however, he was destitute.

Early in that year he became desperately ill and had to be hospitalised.

On his behalf an employee of the railways in Charters Towers, George Foy, wrote to the Minister in charge of the Department of Aboriginal and Torres Strait Islander Affairs saying that Jupiter was in the hospital and not expected to live.

He reported that Jupiter's bank savings were practically exhausted and not sufficient to provide a proper funeral for him.

He went on to ask the Department to provide a sum of 12 pounds for his funeral "in consideration of the native's past service to the community"[27]. A trifling amount, surely, when one considers the millions of dollars in today's

---

[27] Chief Protector of Aboriginals. Memorandum 30 May 1936

money that his discovery of gold had brought to Charters Towers.

A memo from the Protector in Charters Towers to the Chief Protector on 6 June 1936 states that Jupiter had by then been discharged from the General Hospital and that he was "quite alright again" [28]. In addition he notes that "the contract price for the burial of a pauper in Charters Towers is 9 pounds".

By the end of 1936, Jupiter was living in the Eventide home in Charters Towers. The Eventide homes were run by the Salvation Army and provided accommodation for old age pensioners and other elderly persons in need of care.

Jupiter was not entitled to an old-age pension. What happened to the share of his pay that went to the Protector of Aborigines is not documented.

It seems, however, that one of the good citizens of Charters Towers, a Mr J.W. Ward, wrote to E.M. (Ned) Hanlon, then Home Secretary in the Queensland government on Jupiter's behalf and Hanlon was able to put him into the Eventide

---

[28] O'Connor (Protector) to Chief Protector of Aboriginals. Letter 9 June 1936

Home in Charters Towers where he was assured of shelter, a bed, clothes and food.

But this same good citizen was soon again writing, most apologetically, to Hanlon on Jupiter's behalf. Ward tells how he had tried to get public support for Jupiter by advertising in the local press and writing letters.

It worked for a time, but the money soon cut out and "the old fellow had not got a shilling coming in from any source".

This is what Ward asked Hanlon[29] for:

> *I was wondering if you could grant him a few shillings a week either from the Aboriginal fund, or if you could earmark a few shillings from the Golden Casket. An old age pensioner gets 5 shillings a week in addition to his food, clothes, tobacco etc.*
>
> *I must confess it is a bit impertinent of me to ask you to give him 5/- a week, but I was wondering if you could make it 3/- a*

---

[29] Ward, J.W. (1936) Letter to Home Secretary, Mr E.M. Hanlon, 7 November.

week or do something to help the poor old chap.

Just 3/- a week to "help the poor old chap" whose original discovery of gold had put so much wealth into the Queensland government economy.

He got his 3/- a week.

A handwritten note of the 24 October 1941 on Jupiter's file[30] held in the Community and Personal History section of the Department of Aboriginal and Torres Strait Islander Policy and Development says: "This boy receives a pension of 13/- per month. Please advise Superintendent [of Eventide] to submit voucher monthly".

Jupiter died on 5 December 1945.

He was buried in the Charters Towers cemetery and many years later a headstone was erected to mark the site of his grave.

He was thought to have been around 84 when he died.

---

[30] Handwritten note 24 October 1941 Superintendent Eventide Home Charters Towers [re] Pension Jupiter Mosman.

A distinguished gentleman

Up until his death, he was a well-known figure in Charters Towers.

The date of Jupiter's retirement from droving is uncertain. It was sometime in the early 1930s.

I have a cousin who was a regular visitor to Charters Towers. His name was Charlie Shaw.

Charlie, as a young man growing up in the late 1930s and 1940s says he remembers the dignified and very distinguished elderly gentleman, Jupiter Mosman, walking along the streets of Charters Towers.

He may have been on his way to the local cinema or off to visit friends or to see his people in the local community. He would be dressed in his suit and tie wearing his wide-brimmed black stockman's hat.

Jupiter Mosman was well respected and well-liked. This old man had a statesman-like air in his persona and would be greeted by many as he strolled along the street.

Although not a member of the local Gudjal community, he was welcomed among them as an elder and senior man.

The local paper, the *Northern Miner* reported how on the fiftieth anniversary of his death 5 December 1996[31] a large group of people including members of the local Gudjal community held a service at his graveside. The eulogy was appropriately read by Rev. Sr. Edith Edwards of the Good Samaritan Order who trace their links to the Benedictine Order which staffed the college, Lyndhurst, where Jupiter is said to have been sent by Hugh Mosman.

Jupiter was interviewed by Queensland author Jean Devaney in the early 1940s. When asked if he was too old to go prospecting any more he replied:

> *My word, no! I would get away with my packhorses tomorrow if the war was over and I could get stocks. I like prospecting best. I dream of finding gold. But I like cattle and horses, too. I dream of the big drive I once made. Thousands of head of cattle* [32].

A First Nations man, a prospector, a drover, and a man of dignity – that was Jupiter Mosman.

---

[31] Warren, Mark (1996) *Northern Miner* 6 December, 1996, p. 5
[32] Warren, op. cit. p. 5

Is he one of the ghosts of gold who watch over the work of modern miners who resurrect the goldfields that he discovered in the early dawn on that Christmas Eve in 1871?

And now...

In the next and fifth book in this series, *Blood Gold: Native Police, Bushrangers & Lawlessness on the Australian Goldfields* learn about a legacy of the gold discoveries in Australia and how this was manifested in a rise of crime and lawlessness.

Sources

The author would like to acknowledge the following sources of information:

Andrews, T. (1917) Acting Sergeant. Letter.

Australian Prospectors & Miners Hall of Fame "Mosman, Jupiter" http://www.mininghalloffame.com.au/hall-of-fame/inductee.php?id=69

Babidge, S. M. (2004) *Family Affairs: an Historical Anthropology of State Practice and Aboriginal Agency in a Rural Town, North Queensland.* Ph D Thesis.

Babidge, S.M. (2007) *Written True, Not Gammon! A History of Aboriginal Charters Towers.* Thuringowa, Qld., Black Ink Press

Bernays, C.A. (1920) *Queensland Politics During Sixty (1859-1919) Years.* Brisbane, Government Printer.

Black, J. (1952) *North Queensland Pioneers.* Brisbane, Queensland Country Women's Association.

Bolton, G. C. (1970) *A Thousand Miles Away.* Canberra, Australian National University.

Bolton, G.C. "Mosman, Hugh (1843–1909)" in *Australian Dictionary of Biography* https://adb.anu.edu.au/biography/mosman-hugh-4261.

Chief Protector of Aboriginals (1936). Memorandum 30 May.

Chief Protector of Aboriginals.(1923) Memorandum 4 August.

Citigold Corporation https://www.citigold.com/charters-towers-story/

De Satge, O. (1901) *Pages from the Journal of a Queensland Squatter.* London, Hurst and Blackett.

Evans, R., Saunders, K. & Cronin, K. (1988) *Race Relations in Colonial Queensland.* St.Lucia, University of Qld Press

Hill, W.R.O. (1907) *Forty-five Years Experience in North Queensland.* Brisbane, H.Pole.

Holthouse, H. (1970) *Up Rode the Squatter.* Adelaide, Rigby.

Kennedy, M. (1985) *Born a Half-caste.* Canberra, Australian Institute of Aboriginal Studies.

Loos, N. (1982) *Invasion and Resistance.* Canberra, Australian National University.

McKinnon, A. (2019) "Blackbirds: Australia's hidden slave trade history" www.themonthly.com.au/issue/2019/july/1561989600/alex-mckinnon/blackbirds-australias-hidden-slave-trade-history

McLaren, G. (2000) *Big Mobs.* Fremantle, Fremantle Arts Centre.

Marsland, L.W. (1892) *The Charters Towers Gold Mines.* London, Waterlow Bros.

Menghetti, D. (1999) *I Remember: Memories of Charters Towers.* Townsville, James Cook University.

O'Connor (Protector) to Chief Protector of Aboriginals.(1936) Letter 9 June

Palmer, E. (1903) *Early Days in North Queensland.* Sydney, Angus and Robertson.

Pike, G. (1996) *Queensland Frontier.* 3rd ed. Brisbane, G.Pike.

Richards, J. (2008) *The Secret War: a True History of Queensland's Native Police.* Brisbane, University of Queensland Press.

Ryan, W.A. (1917) Sub-Inspector, Protector of Aboriginals. Letter.

Santo, W. (2006) *Gudjal Language Pocket Dictionary.* Black Ink Press.

Stephen, M. D. "Mosman, Archibald (1799–1863)" in *Australian Dictionary of Biography* https://adb.anu.edu.au/biography/mosman-archibald-2485

Ward, J.W. (1936) Letter to Home Secretary, Mr E.M. Hanlon, 7 November.

Warren, M. (1996) *Northern Miner* 6 December.

Questions For Further Consideration

Do First Nations people play a role in gold mining today?

Do First Nations people get royalties from gold mining today?

Has gold mining in Australia positively impacted First Nations people at all?

About Marji Hill

Artist & Author

Marji Hill, artist and painter since childhood, runs her art career alongside her career as an author.

Marji is a highly respected international author as well as a seasoned business executive, researcher, and coach.

She is passionate about promoting understanding between Australia's first people and other Australians.

Marji has fostered the spirit of reconciliation in all her writings since she was Research Fellow in Education at the Australian Institute of Aboriginal and Torres Strait Islander Studies (AIATSIS) in Canberra.

Gold! Hidden Stories of Australia s Past, Book 4

From 2008 to 2011, Marji was Deputy Chairperson of the Mosman Branch of Reconciliation Australia in Sydney.

Following her Education Research Fellowship at AIATSIS in 1976 Marji, together with her late partner, Alex Barlow, produced more than seventy (70) books on all aspects of the First Nations people including the critical, annotated bibliography *Black Australia*.

In 1989 Marji was the Project Coordinator and one of the researchers and writers of *Australian Aboriginal Culture* the official Australian Government publication on First Nations people.

In 1988 her work of non-fiction *Six Australian Battlefields*, which she co-authored with Al Grassby, was published by Angus and Robertson. A decade later it was re-published by Allen & Unwin as a paperback edition.

Her nine-volume encyclopaedia, *Macmillan Encyclopaedia of Australia's Aboriginal Peoples* was published in 2000 and in 2009 she published *The Apology: Saying Sorry to the Stolen Generations*.

Marji's more recent publications extend to self-improvement and self-help with books like *Staying*

Young Growing Old and *Inspired by Country* a self-help book about painting with gouache.

Marji's artworks range from very large oil paintings on canvas (her largest being 213 x 167cm) to very small works on paper - gouache being a favourite medium.

Black/white relations, reconciliation, Eureka, and the discovery of gold are common themes not only in her writings but also in her art.

Her small paintings are simple responses to land and sea environments.

Painting has been a lifetime passion for Marji. She remembers as a child winning first prize for a painting she exhibited at the Southport agricultural show. Then in her teens for two years in a row she won the Sunday Mail Child Art Competition in Queensland with her winning paintings getting full coverage in colour in the newspaper.

Marji's formal art training took place in the 1980s at the Canberra School of Art which in 1992 became ANU School of Art & Design.

As soon as she completed her Master of Arts Degree in Anthropology at the Australian National University (ANU), Marji went on to get a Post

Graduate Diploma in Painting. She has held eight solo exhibitions in Canberra, Melbourne and Sydney and she has participated in various group shows.

One of her large paintings was included in the 2004- 2005 Art Gallery of Ballarat Travelling Exhibition *Eureka Revisited: the Contest of Memories*. This exhibition travelled to Melbourne, Canberra and Ballarat - part of the 150-year celebration of the Eureka Stockade.

Two of her large paintings were commissioned by the Citigold Corporation. One did hang for many years in the foyer of Jupiter's Casino in Townsville until the casino was sold, becoming the Ville Resort-Casino.

Jupiter's Lucky Strike celebrates the discovery of gold by First Nations boy, Jupiter Mosman in 1871 at Charters Towers in North Queensland. This painting today hangs in the offices of the Citigold Corporation in Charters Towers.

The other, a portrait of Jupiter Mosman resides in the World Theatre in Charters Towers.

Marji's paintings are in many private collections both in Australia and overseas and she is represented in the Art Gallery of Ballarat and the

Ballarat and Sydney campuses of the Australian Catholic University.

For many years Marji travelled extensively both within Australia and internationally, working as a consultant, doing speaking engagements, motivating people, and developing her art career.

Marji has returned to her birthplace and now resides in Surfers Paradise. She pursues her interests of writing, painting, mentoring, publishing, and internet marketing.

More Books by Marji Hill

Self-improvement/Self-Help

Hill, Marji (2014) *Staying Young Growing Old.* Broadbeach, Qld, The Prison Tree Press.

Hill, Marji (2020) *How Big Is Your Why? An Author's Guide to Time Management and Productivity to Achieve Transformational Results.* Broadbeach, Qld, The Prison Tree Press.

Hill, Marji (2020) *A Create and Publish Toolbox: 101 Prompts in A Guided Journal To Help You Write, Self-publish, and Market Your Book On Amazon.* Broadbeach, Qld, The Prison Tree Press.

Hill, Marji (2021) *Inspired by Country: an Artist's Journey Back to Nature, Landscape Painting with Gouache.* Broadbeach, Qld, The Prison Tree Press.

First Nations

Hill, Marji (2021) *First People Then And Now: Introducing Indigenous Australians.* 2nd ed. Broadbeach, Qld, The Prison Tree Press.

Hill, Marji (2021) *Australian Aboriginal History: 5 Stories of Indigenous Heroes.* Broadbeach, Qld, The Prison Tree Press.

Gold

Hill, Marji (2022) *Gates of Gold: The Discovery of Gold, its Legacy and its Contribution to Australian Identity.* Broadbeach, Qld, The Prison Tree Press.

Hill, Marji (2022) *Shadows of Gold: Eureka and the Birth of Australian Democracy.* Broadbeach, Qld, The Prison Tree Press.

Hill, Marji (2022) *Gold and the Chinese: Racism, Riots and Protest on the Australian Goldfields.* Broadbeach, Qld, The Prison Tree Press.

Hill, Marji (2022) *Ghosts of Gold: The Life and Times of Jupiter Mosman.* Broadbeach, Qld, The Prison Tree Press.

Hill, Marji (2022) *Blood Gold: Native Police, Bushrangers & Lawlessness on the Australian Goldfields.* Broadbeach, Qld, The Prison Tree Press.

For a more complete listing of her works, please visit Marji's website:

https://marjihill.com

Gold! Hidden Stories of Australia s Past,
Book 4

www.ingramcontent.com/pod-product-compliance
Lightning Source LLC
Chambersburg PA
CBHW041459010526
44107CB00044B/1507